St. Mary's Abbey Gate, Colchester

ESSEX RECIPES

compiled by
Michelle Carter

with illustrations by
L. Burleigh Bruhl RBA

SALMON

*I*NDEX

Asparagus Pudding 27
Barley Cream Soup 6
Chelmsford Pudding 45
Colchester Pudding 23
Colne Chicken 7
Courting Cake 47
Cranham Honey Cake 31
Cressing Biscuits 19
Debden Tomato and
    Apple Chutney 40
Devilled Whitebait 11
Essex Apple Slices 24
Essex Cockle Soup 46
Essex Hotpot 37
Essex Meat Layer Pudding 21
Essex Pudding Pies 8
Essex Pumpkin Pie 30
Essex Scrap-cakes 39

Essex Shortcakes 3
Kitchels 13
Leek Pudding 42
Maldon Boiled Beef 29
Onion Pudding 34
Pheasant with
    D'Arcy Spice Apples 18
Pigeon and Parsnip Casserole 5
Potted Ham 22
Roast Pork with Walnut Stuffing 43
Saffron Cake 16
Sautéed Pigeon Breasts 35
Smoked Oyster Parcels 15
Southend Fruit Shells 14
Stuffed Lettuce Hearts 26
Stuffed Whole Plaice 38
Tipsy D'Arcy Spice Apples 32
Ugley Duckling 10

Cover pictures: *front:* The King's Head, Chigwell, by A. R. Quinton
back: Cockles – Leigh Creek
Printed and Published by J. Salmon Ltd., Sevenoaks, England ©

Essex Shortcakes

9 oz. self raising flour
2 oz. sugar
3 oz. margarine
1 oz. lard
1½ oz. currants
1 fl. oz. milk
Sugar for sprinkling

Set oven to 400°F or Mark 6. Sift the flour into bowl and add the sugar. Rub in the fats, then add the currants. Gradually mix in the milk until the mixture binds together. Gently roll out the mixture to ½-inch thick on a lightly floured surface and then cut into slices. Place on a greased baking tray and sprinkle sugar over the top of the biscuits. Bake for about 10 minutes until pale golden brown. Remove the biscuits from the baking sheet while still warm and transfer to a wire rack to cool. Makes about 12-16 slices.

These shortcake biscuits contain currants and are sprinkled with sugar before baking.

Little Dunmow

Pigeon and Parsnip Casserole

4 pigeons, plucked and dressed
2 small parsnips
4 oz. unsmoked streaky bacon, chopped
2 onions, chopped
2 oz. butter
1 dessertspoon flour
Salt and pepper
Bunch of herbs

Blanch the parsnips in boiling salted water for a few minutes. Drain, cut into slices and set aside and keep the water. In a pan, sauté the pigeons in the butter until brown on all sides. Add the chopped bacon and chopped onions. Then sprinkle with flour. Mix well and add the parsnip cooking water and the sliced parsnips. Season, add the herbs and cook over a low heat until tender. Serve with creamed potatoes and a green vegetable. Serves 4.

Barley Cream Soup

4 oz. pearl barley
1¾ pints chicken stock
¼ pint milk
¼ pint double cream
Salt and pepper
1 oz. butter
2 teaspoons chopped parsley

Blanch the barley by placing in a bowl and pouring on boiling water. Leave for 1 minute and then drain. Add the drained barley to the chicken stock in a saucepan and simmer for 2 hours. Liquidise the barley mixture and then add to it the milk, cream, salt and pepper, and the butter cut up into small pieces. Return to the saucepan, reheat and then serve sprinkled with the chopped parsley. Serves 6.

A recipe from the 18th century when Essex was a considerable barley growing county.

Colne Chicken

4 chicken breasts, boned and skinned
8 rashers of streaky bacon
Juice of one lemon
½ tablespoon chopped sage
1 tablespoon chopped parsley
1 tablespoon chopped thyme
Grated rind of one lemon

Set the grill to hot. Flatten the chicken breasts with a wet knife and cut in half lengthways. Brush the chicken pieces with lemon juice. Mix together all the herbs and sprinkle each piece of chicken with the herbs and lemon rind. Wrap a rasher of streaky bacon around each piece of chicken and grill until cooked. Serve two pieces of chicken to each person with roast or sauté potatoes and a green vegetable. Serves 4.

A grilled chicken dish from the villages in the Colne Valley.

Essex Pudding Pies

1½ oz. ground rice
¾ pint milk
1½ oz. butter
2 oz. sugar
3 eggs
Pinch of salt
Grated nutmeg
3 oz. currants
8 oz. shortcrust pastry

Set oven to 400°F or Mark 6. In a saucepan, boil the ground rice in the milk for 15 minutes. Remove from the heat and stir in the butter and the sugar. Beat the eggs well and add them to the rice mixture together with the salt and nutmeg. Beat well and leave to cool, but not set. Roll out the pastry on a lightly floured surface and use it to line 8 small, greased 6 oz. pudding basins. Fill each basin ¾-full with the rice mixture and sprinkle with currants on top. Bake for 15 minutes. Serves about 6.

A rice and custard dish which is baked as individual puddings.

Dedham from the Stour

Ugley Duckling

1 large duck, about 6 lb.
Juice of 1 orange
2 oz. shredded suet
4 oz. soft breadcrumbs
Pinch grated nutmeg
3 teaspoons chopped parsley
1 teaspoon mixed herbs
Grated zest of an orange
Salt and pepper
Duck liver, chopped
Two rashers of streaky bacon, chopped
1 egg
Orange segments and rashers of streaky bacon for garnish

Set oven to 425°F or Mark 7. Prick the duck breast with a skewer, brush over with the orange juice and sprinkle with salt. Make the stuffing by mixing the breadcrumbs with the suet, add the nutmeg, parsley, mixed herbs and orange zest. Then add the chopped duck liver and chopped bacon rashers. Season. Beat the egg and mix it with the stuffing mixture to bind it. Stuff the duck and place on the highest shelf of the oven for half an hour. Now reduce the oven heat to 350°F, or Mark 4 and roast for a further 2 hours. Transfer to a serving dish, garnish with the segments of orange that have been wrapped in the streaky bacon rashers and then fried. Serves 4.

Roast duck with a delicious herb stuffing from the village of Ugley near Saffron Walden.

Devilled Whitebait

1 lb. whitebait
4 tablespoons flour
2 teaspoons curry powder
½ teaspoon chilli powder
Black pepper
Lemon wedges
Oil for frying

Wash the whitebait, dry well on kitchen paper and set aside. Put the flour with the other dry ingredients in a bowl and mix well. Heat the oil very hot in a deep pan. Coat the whitebait in the seasoned flour and fry in the oil, a few at a time, until crisp (about 2-3 minutes). Remove with a slotted spoon and drain on crumpled kitchen paper. Keep the batches of cooked whitebait hot in the oven until they are all cooked. Serve with thick lemon wedges and buttered brown bread. Serves 4.

Every year a blessing of the first whitebait catch is held at Southend. This fish is caught in large numbers along the South Essex coast.

The Old Tide Mill, Walton-on-the-Naze

Kitchels

1 lb. puff pastry
2 oz. butter
8 oz. currants
3 oz. chopped mixed peel
2 oz. ground almonds
½ teaspoon ground cinnamon
½ teaspoon ground nutmeg
Sugar for sprinkling

Set oven to 425°F or Mark 7. Divide the pastry in half and roll each piece into a thin square on a lightly floured surface. Melt the butter in a saucepan and mix in the currants, peel, almonds and spices. Spread this filling mixture evenly on one of the pastry squares to within ½-inch of the edges, moisten the edges with water and cover with the second piece of pastry. Press together and seal the edges. Mark the top into 2 inch squares without cutting through. Bake for 25 minutes until well risen and golden brown. Sprinkle with caster sugar and divide whilst still warm.

It was the custom for the newly-elected Mayor of Harwich to throw kitchels from the window of the Guildhall to the children in the street below.

Southend Fruit Shells

4 oz. butter
4 oz. caster sugar
2 eggs
6 oz. flour
1 teaspoon baking powder
Few drops vanilla essence
1 fl. oz. milk
3 oz. raspberries
3 oz. blackcurrants
Juice of 1 lemon
1 tablespoon sugar
Fruit leaves
Scallop shells or pyrex shell-shaped dishes

Set oven to 350°F or Mark 4. In a bowl, cream together the butter and sugar. Beat the eggs well and gradually add to the creamed mixture. Sift the flour and baking powder together and fold into the mixture. Add the vanilla essence and enough milk to form a soft, dropping consistency. Grease the shells and divide the sponge mixture between them. Cook for 15 minutes or until well risen and golden brown. Meanwhile stew the fruit with the sugar and lemon juice. Allow to cool. When the sponge shells have cooled, slice into the sponge lengthways, but not all the way through, part the edges and fill with the stewed fruit. Decorate with fruit leaves. Makes about 6-8 shells.

Smoked Oyster Parcels

3 x 4 oz. cans smoked oysters
3 hardboiled eggs, peeled and finely chopped
5 oz. fresh brown breadcrumbs
1 teaspoon fresh or dried dill, chopped
Salt and pepper
12 medium sized spinach leaves

Cut the oysters in half and place in a bowl with their juice. Add the finely chopped hard-boiled eggs, breadcrumbs and dill and blend together. Season. Wash the spinach leaves and remove most of the stems. Steam them for exactly one minute and cool under cold running water. Pat dry each leaf with kitchen paper. Place two teaspoons of the stuffing mixture on to the stem end of a spinach leaf, roll over once, then fold in the sides and roll again to the end so that you have a small, enclosed sausage. Repeat with all the leaves. Then steam the parcels for 10 minutes and serve hot as a starter. Serves 4.

Colchester is the centre of Essex oyster growing and the ancient Colchester Oyster Feast is held in October.

Saffron Cake

12 oz. self raising flour
8 oz. currants
4 oz. butter
2 eggs
¼ pint milk
4 oz. sultanas
2 oz. candied peel
3 oz. brown sugar
¼ teaspoon saffron

Set oven to 350°F or Mark 4. Put the saffron into the milk in a bowl to extract the flavour and stand in the oven for 30 minutes; remove from oven and set aside to cool. Meanwhile, cream together in a bowl the butter and sugar, mix in the flour and then the currants and sultanas. Beat in the eggs and the saffron milk. Mix well and put the mixture into a greased 9-inch round cake tin and bake in the oven for 1½ hours until golden brown.

The purple-petalled autumn flowering crocus which gave the town of Saffron Walden the first part of its name was widely cultivated in the locality until the end of the 18th century for culinary and cloth-dying purposes. The yellow saffron is obtained from the crocus stamens.

Audley End near Saffron Walden

*P*HEASANT WITH D'ARCY SPICE APPLES

1 pheasant
2¼ lbs. D'Arcy Spice apples
2 oz. butter
1 onion, chopped
4 juniper berries
Pinch of thyme
1 bayleaf
1 glass of apple juice
Salt and pepper to taste

Peel and core the apples, leave them whole and set aside. In a large saucepan, sauté the pheasant in the butter until golden brown on all sides. Add the chopped onion, herbs, berries, seasoning and apple juice and surround with the apples. Cover, bring to the boil then simmer until the pheasant is tender. Boil down the pan juices and thicken with a little cornflour, if preferred, to make the gravy. Serve with roast potatoes or game chips and a green vegetable. Serves 2.

If D'Arcy Spice apples are not available, then Egremont Russet will make a satisfactory alternative.

Cressing Biscuits

4 oz. flour
3 oz. sugar
2 oz. margarine
2 oz. lard
1 cup rolled oats
½ teaspoon bicarbonate of soda
1 teaspoon baking powder
1 teaspoon hot water
1 teaspoon golden syrup

BUTTER CREAM
5 oz. icing sugar
3 oz. margarine
Vanilla essence

Plain biscuits filled with a butter cream from Cressing near Braintree.

Set oven to 350°F or Mark 4. In a bowl cream together the margarine, lard and sugar. Sift the flour together with the bicarbonate of soda and the baking powder and mix into the creamed mixture, together with the oats, syrup and hot water. Form into 24 walnut size balls and cook, well spaced, on a greased baking sheet for 10-15 minutes. Transfer to a wire rack to cool. Make up the butter cream by beating together the icing sugar, margarine and a little vanilla essence and use to sandwich the biscuits when cold.

In the heart of Epping Forest

Essex Meat Layer Pudding

SUET PASTRY
6 oz. flour
¼ teaspoon salt
3 oz. shredded suet
¼ cup cold water

FILLING
1 tablespoon butter
2 medium sized onions, sliced
½ lb. minced pork
½ lb. minced veal or chicken
1 teaspoon dried sage
¼ teaspoon dried oregano
1 tablespoon chopped chives
¼ teaspoon black pepper
½ teaspoon salt
¼ teaspoon celery salt
1 tablespoon flour
2 egg yolks
2 tablespoons double cream

Pastry: sift flour and salt into bowl and mix in suet. Add enough water to make a stiff dough. Wrap and put in refrigerator for 10 minutes. Meanwhile make filling. Fry onions in butter until soft and golden. Add meats, herbs, seasonings and flour; mix well, cook for 5 minutes then remove pan from heat. Beat together egg yolks and cream and add to meat mixture. Cook 5 minutes more. Butter 2½ pint pudding basin. Roll out dough on a floured surface to ¼-inch thick. Cut small circle to fit bottom of basin and put in place. Spoon on layer of meat mixture (about 1½-inches deep) then add another circle of dough to fit and another layer of meat. Continue until filling and dough have been used up, finishing with layer of dough (3 layers of meat mixture). Ingredients will not fill basin, but need room for dough to expand. Cover basin with greaseproof paper and kitchen foil and steam for 4 hours. Turn out on to a plate and serve with vegetables. Serves 4.

Potted Ham

2 tablespoons vegetable oil
8 oz. onion, peeled and sliced thinly
1 lb. cooked ham
½ teaspoon cayenne pepper
½ oz. curry powder
1 teaspoon paprika
Salt
¼ pint cider or red wine
2 oz. butter

Heat the oil in a frying pan and add the onions. Fry until tender, but not browned. Finely mince the ham and onions together. Add the spices and mix well together. Add salt to taste. Put the cider or red wine into a saucepan and add the ham mixture. Mix well and simmer over a low heat for 30 minutes. Remove from the heat and allow to cool. Pack the mixture into stone, pottery or glass jars. Melt the butter in a saucepan over a low heat. Skim off the foam and strain the yellow liquid into a bowl, leaving the milky residue in the pan. Pour the clarified butter on to the surface of the ham mixture to seal and cover with paper covers.

This potted ham, from an 18th century recipe, will keep for two months in the refrigerator if the seal is unbroken.

Colchester Pudding

1¾ pints milk
1½ oz. tapioca
Pinch of salt
Grated lemon rind
Vanilla essence
1 lb. stewed fruit, as available in season
6 egg yolks
½ lb. caster sugar
5 fl. oz. double cream
3 egg whites

A pudding containing tapioca and stewed fruit topped with meringue.

Heat oven to 400°F or Mark 6. Heat 1 pint of the milk in a pan, sprinkle on tapioca and salt and bring to the boil. Simmer gently until soft. After 10 minutes add the lemon rind and a few drops of vanilla essence. Put a layer of stewed fruit in an ovenproof dish and cover with the tapioca. To make the rich custard, heat the milk slowly in a saucepan until just simmering; remove from heat. Meanwhile mix the egg yolks and 3 oz of the sugar in a bowl. Gradually whisk the cooled milk into the egg mixture, return to the saucepan over a gentle heat, whisking all the time until it thickens. Then stir in the cream and pour the custard over the tapioca. Next whisk egg whites until stiff, spoon in remaining sugar and pipe meringue mixture over the custard. Put in the oven and bake until the top is brown. Serves 4-6.

Essex Apple Slices

1 medium cooking apple
Juice of ½ lemon
½ lb. self raising flour
¼ teaspoon baking powder
Pinch of salt
4 oz. margarine
4 oz. caster sugar
¼ pint milk
1 egg
A little melted fat

ICING
½ lb. sifted icing sugar
3 teaspoons lemon juice

Set oven to 375°F or Mark 5. Peel, core and chop the apple finely and mix with the lemon juice. Sift the flour, salt and baking powder into a bowl and rub in the margarine. Beat the milk and egg together and stir thoroughly into the mixture together with the chopped apple. Brush an 11 x 7 inch shallow baking tin with melted fat. Pour the mixture into the tin and spread evenly. Bake for 45 minutes. Make the icing by mixing the icing sugar with the lemon juice and just enough water to make a thick spreading consistency. Pour the icing on to the top of the cake whilst still warm and spread evenly. Allow to cool in the tin and when cold cut into 16 slices.

A sponge cake topped with lemon icing and cut into slices.

Passingford Mill on the Roding

Stuffed Lettuce Hearts

6 oz. cooked pork, skinned and cubed
2 hardboiled eggs, peeled and finely chopped
¼ teaspoon ground mace
½ teaspoon salt
¼ teaspoon pepper
2 oz. softened butter
1 tablespoon chopped parsley and chives mixed
8 crisp heart-leaves of lettuce
½ cucumber, peeled and finely sliced
2 oz. finely chopped walnuts

Mix together the pork, eggs, mace, salt and pepper and stir into the softened butter in a bowl. Add the chopped parsley and chives and mix well. Arrange the cucumber slices on four small plates. Divide the stuffing into 8 equal amounts and fill each lettuce leaf with a portion of the stuffing. Put 2 leaves on each plate with the cucumber. Sprinkle with walnuts and chill in the refrigerator for not more than 2 hours. Serves 4.

An old recipe for lettuce leaves filled with a pork, egg and herb stuffing

Asparagus Pudding

2 dessertspoons minced ham
4 eggs, beaten
1 dessertspoon flour
Salt and pepper
A knob of butter
½ lb. asparagus
A few tarragon leaves, chopped

Mince the ham finely and in a bowl, combine with the well-beaten eggs, flour, salt and pepper and the butter. Cut the top part of the asparagus spears into very small pieces and, together with the chopped tarragon, mix with the other ingredients. Then add enough milk to produce a thick, creamy consistency. Pour into a well-buttered mould or pudding basin, cover in foil and steam for 2 hours. Turn out on to a warmed serving dish and pour melted butter round the pudding. Serve hot with hot buttered toast. Serves 4.

This 19th century Essex recipe makes a delicate first course.

Hay barges on the Blackwater

Maldon Boiled Beef

1 piece of topside or silverside of beef
1 carrot
1 onion, peeled
1 leek
Bunch of herbs
2 cloves
Peppercorns
Water
Maldon Crystal Salt

Peel the onion and stud with the cloves. Scrub the carrot, wash the leek and place with the meat and all the other ingredients, except the salt, in a saucepan. Cover with water, bring to the boil and simmer until the meat is cooked and tender. Lift the meat out of the stock on to a serving dish. Serve the meat sliced, with a good grinding of Maldon Crystal Sea Salt over each slice, together with accompanying vegetables. The stock can be used for soup. Serves 4.

A warming meal made with the famous Maldon Sea Salt.

Essex Pumpkin Pie

1 lb. ripe pumpkin, diced
½ lb. apple, diced
½ lb. currants
½ lb. sultanas
4 oz. brown sugar
1 teaspoon mixed spice
1 teaspoon ground ginger
Juice of a lemon
¾ lb. shortcrust pastry
Egg white for brushing
Sugar for sprinkling

Set oven to 400°F or Mark 6. Mix together in a bowl all the ingredients and put the mixture into a large pie dish; oval or round about 9 inches in diameter and 1½-2 inches deep. Roll out the pastry on a lightly floured surface and cover the pumpkin mixture. Brush with egg white and sprinkle with sugar. Put in the oven and bake for 20 minutes. Then reduce the temperature to 350°F or Mark 4 and bake for a further 20 minutes, or until the pastry is golden brown. Serves 6.

An Autumn pudding containing pumpkin, apple and dried fruit.

Cranham Honey Cake

½ lb. self-raising flour
2 eggs
5 oz. margarine
2½ oz. caster sugar
3 oz. thick honey
Grated lemon rind
2 oz. glacé cherries, chopped
Pinch of salt
4 tablespoons milk

Set oven to 375°F or Mark 5. Cream together in a bowl the margarine, sugar and honey. Beat the eggs and then beat them into the mixture. Fold in the sieved flour, salt, cherries and lemon rind. Add the milk and mix well. Turn into a greased and floured 7 inch round cake tin. Bake for one hour until golden brown. Allow to cool in the tin before turning out.

Tipsy D'Arcy Spice Apples

2 lb. D'Arcy spice apples
4 oz. soft brown sugar
3 oz. unsalted butter
1 large glass sweet white wine

Set oven to 450°F or Mark 8. Butter an 11 inch oval, ovenproof dish. Core and slice, but do not peel, the apples. Lay the apple slices in the dish with the slices overlapping. Sprinkle on the sugar and dot with small pieces of the butter. Pour the wine over the top and bake until tender. Serve with single cream. Serves 6.

The D'Arcy Spice apple was first found in the garden of the Hall at Tolleshunt D'Arcy in 1880; they are a late russet variety which is picked in November and keeps until May. If D'Arcy Spice apples are not available, then Egremont Russet will make a satisfactory alternative.

Layer Marney Towers

Onion Pudding

½ lb. self raising flour
4 oz. shredded suet
Salt and pepper
1 dessertspoon mixed herbs
1 lb. onions, peeled and chopped
Milk and water to mix

In a bowl, mix together the dry ingredients and form a soft dough with the milk and water. Mix in the onions. Put the mixture into a greased pudding basin, cover with greased paper and a cloth or kitchen foil and steam for 2-2½ hours. This pudding is delicious eaten hot with boiled ham or boiled beef. Serves 4-6.

A soft, dough pudding with onions and herbs that is excellent on its own or as an accompaniment to boiled meat.

S*autéed* P*igeon* B*reasts*

8 pigeon breasts
2 oz. butter
1 large glass of white wine
1 onion, peeled and chopped
1 garlic clove, chopped
2 sticks celery, chopped
Salt and pepper
2 sprigs tarragon

In a pan, sauté the pigeon breasts in the butter until golden brown on all sides. Add the wine, onion, garlic and chopped celery. Season, cover the pan and simmer for 20 minutes. Add the tarragon and continue to simmer, uncovered, for a further 15 minutes. Serve with mashed potatoes and a green vegetable. Serves 4.

Cooked with celery, this dish is a favourite with rough shooters.

Winter on the Roach

Essex Hotpot

1½ lb. lean pork, cubed
2 medium onions, peeled and sliced
1 can condensed chicken soup
1 small can peeled tomatoes
6 medium potatoes, peeled and sliced
3 oz. Cheddar cheese, grated
Oil for frying

Set oven to 350°F or Mark 4. Remove any bones from the meat and cut into chunky cubes. Fry the onion in a little oil until soft, mix in the meat cubes and brown them quickly on all sides. Transfer to an oven-proof casserole. Add the soup and tomatoes and season to taste. Cover with the sliced potatoes and sprinkle the grated cheese over the top. Cover with foil and cook in the oven for 2-2½ hours. Remove the foil for the last 20 minutes. Serve with a green vegetable. Serves 6.

A quickly made pork hotpot covered with potato and cheese.

Stuffed Whole Plaice

4 small plaice (about 12 oz. each)
4 oz. Cheddar cheese
2 oz. white breadcrumbs
1 teaspoon dry mustard
2 teaspoons parsley
Juice of ½ a lemon
1 egg, beaten

Set oven to 375°F or Mark 5. Make a cut lengthwise down the centre of each fish and loosen the flesh on both sides of the cut to form a pocket. To make the stuffing, grate the cheese and mix with the breadcrumbs, mustard, parsley, lemon juice and beaten egg. Spoon the stuffing into the pocket of each fish. Place the fish in a buttered baking dish, dot with butter and cover with kitchen foil. Bake for 20-30 minutes. Serves 4.

In this recipe the whole fish is filled with a cheese and mushroom stuffing.

Essex Scrap Cakes

1½-2 lb. flead (producing approx. 6 oz. of "scraps")
1 lb. flour
4 oz. light soft brown sugar
1 teaspoon ground allspice
1 oz. candied lemon peel
6 oz. currants
Milk to mix
¼ teaspoon bicarbonate of soda

These cakes are very wholesome for children and the resulting home-made lard is of generally better quality than the mass-produced product.

To make the "scraps" take the flead (the fat from the inside of a pig), remove the skin membrane and cut it into small pieces. Place in an ovenproof dish in a hot oven until the fat is reduced to oil, leaving small pieces, or "scraps" floating on the surface. Take care not to let it get too hot; the "scraps" should be crispy but not browned. Strain off the molten lard and set aside to solidify for future use. Set oven to 425°F or Mark 7. In a bowl, rub the cold scraps into the flour and add the sugar, spice, peel and currants. Mix the bicarbonate of soda with the milk and beat well into the mixture to make a thick paste. Spoon into greased small Yorkshire Pudding tins (or similar). Bake for 15-20 minutes until golden brown. Makes about 25-30 cakes.

Debden Tomato and Apple Chutney

2 lb. Bramley apples
1 lb. red tomatoes
½ lb. moist brown sugar
2 oz. onion, chopped
1 pint vinegar
½ lb. raisins
1 teaspoon salt
Pinch of cayenne pepper

Peel, slice and core the apples. In a saucepan, cook together the sliced apples, tomatoes, onions, and raisins in the vinegar until soft. Add the sugar, salt and pepper and cook for about a further 20 minutes. The mixture is sufficiently reduced when a channel formed by a wooden spoon drawn through the mixture no longer fills with vinegar. Pot into hot, sterilised jars and seal with plastic lids or jampot covers. Store for at least one month before eating.

A tangy, Bramley apple chutney from the village of Debden midway between Saffron Walden and Thaxted.

The Guildhall and Church, Thaxted

Leek Pudding

6 oz. leeks
8 oz. flour
1 teaspoon baking powder
3 oz. shredded suet
4 fl. oz. cold water
½ teaspoon salt

Wash and dry the leeks and cut them into thin round slices. Sift together the flour, salt and baking powder into a bowl and add the suet. Mix to a firm dough with cold water. On a lightly floured surface roll out the dough into a rectangle about ¼-inch thick. Spread the leeks liberally over the dough and sprinkle with salt to taste. Roll up from a short end, wrap in a clean pudding cloth and tie each end with string. Place in a saucepan of boiling water and simmer for 1½-2 hours. This pudding is delicious served with Maldon Boiled Beef. Serves 4-6.

A traditional boiled suet pudding filled with leeks to accompany boiled or casseroled meats.

Roast Pork with Walnut & Spinach Stuffing

3 lb. spare rib of pork, boned
4 oz. spinach
1 oz. butter
1 onion, chopped
4 rashers of smoked streaky bacon, chopped
3 oz. cooked long grain rice
2 oz. chopped walnuts
1 egg
1 tablespoon double cream
Salt and pepper

Set oven to 350°F or Mark 4. Wash the spinach and remove the stalks. Boil for 2 minutes in very little water, drain well and chop. Set aside and keep hot. Melt the butter in small pan, add the chopped onion and cook for 5 minutes. Add the chopped bacon and fry until cooked. Remove from the heat and stir in all the other ingredients and the spinach and season. Mix well and stuff the pocket in the pork left by the removal of the blade bone. Roll up and tie round with string. Roast for 2 hours. Serve sliced, with vegetables. Serves 8.

Roast spare rib of pork with an unusual and delicious local stuffing.

Baddow Road Mill near Chelmsford

Chelmsford Pudding

2 oz. butter
2 oz. sugar
1 egg
¼ pint milk
4 oz. self raising flour
Pinch of salt
6 oz. stewed fruit, as available in season
Sugar for sprinkling

Set oven to 350°F or Mark 4. In a bowl, beat the butter and sugar to a cream. In another bowl, beat the egg and add the milk to it. Add the flour and milk/egg mixture alternately to the butter/sugar mixture. Beat well. Add salt. Arrange the stewed fruit in a greased 2 pint pie dish and pour the sponge mixture over. Bake for 30-40 minutes. Remove from the oven and sprinkle the top with sugar. Serve hot with custard. Serves 4.

This baked dessert is made with stewed fruit according to the season.

Essex Cockle Soup

4 slices smoked streaky bacon, chopped
4 tomatoes
4 medium new potatoes
2 onions, peeled and chopped
1 large glass dry white wine
Water
Black pepper
Tablespoon chopped parsley
2 pints of cockles in their shells

Fry the bacon until crisp then set aside. Peel the tomatoes by placing them in hot water for 5 minutes, then chop roughly. Peel and dice the potatoes. Fry the potatoes, onions and tomatoes in the bacon fat. When the onions are transparent add the wine, bring to the boil and transfer to a large saucepan. Add sufficient water to cover the mixture, season with pepper and simmer until the potatoes are tender. Meanwhile, clean the cockles thoroughly, place in a saucepan with a little water, cover and cook until they open. Remove the cockles from their shells and put together with their cooking liquor into the soup pan. Serve at once, topped with the bacon and the chopped parsley. Serves 4.

Leigh-on-Sea is the centre of the Essex cockle industry.

Courting Cake

SPONGE MIXTURE
3 eggs
3 oz. caster sugar
3 oz. flour
Pinch of salt
Pinch of baking powder

SWEET SHORTCRUST PASTRY
6 oz. flour
3 oz. margarine
1 tablespoon sugar
1 egg

FRUIT FILLING
1 lb. cooking apples peeled and chopped
1 oz. sugar
1 tablespoon lemon juice

BUTTER ICING
4 oz. icing sugar, 1 oz. butter

Set oven to 375°F or Mark 5. *Sponge mixture:* whisk the eggs and sugar together in a bowl until thick and creamy. Sift and fold in the flour, salt and baking powder with a metal spoon. *Pastry:* rub the fat into the flour, then add the sugar, bind with the egg and, if needed, a little water. *Fruit filling:* cook the apples with the sugar and lemon juice. Roll out the pastry on a lightly floured surface and use to line a 9 inch deep cake tin. Pour in the apple filling and then pour the sponge mixture on top of the apples. Cook for 25-35 minutes. Allow to cool in the tin. *Butter icing:* beat together the icing sugar and butter until smooth and creamy and use to spread over the cake when cold.

METRIC CONVERSIONS

The weights, measures and oven temperatures used in the preceding recipes can be easily converted to their metric equivalents.

Weights

Avoirdupois	Metric
1 oz.	just under 30 grams
4 oz. (¼ lb.)	app. 115 grams
8 oz. (½ lb.)	app. 230 grams
1 lb.	454 grams

Liquid Measures

Imperial	Metric
1 tablespoon (liquid only)	20 millilitres
1 fl. oz.	app. 30 millilitres
1 gill (¼ pt.)	app. 145 millilitres
½ pt.	app. 285 millilitres
1 pt.	app. 570 millilitres
1 qt.	app. 1.140 litres

Oven Temperatures

	°Fahrenheit	Gas Mark	°Celsius
Slow	300	2	140
	325	3	158
Moderate	350	4	177
	375	5	190
	400	6	204
Hot	425	7	214
	450	8	232
	500	9	260

Flour as specified in these recipes refers to Plain Flour unless otherwise described.